FOR SPENDING YOUR MONEY WISELY

BARBARA GOTTFRIED HOLLANDER

ROSEN PUBLISHING®

New York

This book is dedicated to Rose Cohen, who does everything wisely

Published in 2014 by The Rosen Publishing Group, Inc.
29 East 21st Street, New York, NY 10010

Library of Congress Cataloging-in-Publication Data

Hollander, Barbara Gottfried.
Top 10 secrets for spending your money wisely/by Barbara Gottfried Hollander.
    p. cm.—(A student's guide to financial empowerment)
Includes bibliographical references and index.
ISBN 978-1-4488-9361-4 (library binding)—
ISBN 978-1-4488-9380-5 (pbk.)—
ISBN 978-1-4488-9381-2 (6-pack)
1. Consumption (Economics)—Juvenile literature. 2. Money—Juvenile literature. 3. Finance, Personal—Juvenile literature. I. Hollander, Barbara Gottfried. II. Title.
HC79.C6 H6535 2014
332.024—d23

Manufactured in the United States of America

CPSIA Compliance Information: Batch #S13YA: For further information, contact Rosen Publishing, New York, New York, at 1-800-237-9932.

Contents

Teens use cash, debit cards, and credit cards to purchase goods and services. It's important to use all of these tools wisely.

Introduction

Money does not grow on trees. It is a limited commodity used to meet some of people's most basic needs, including clothes, food, and shelter. Today relatives pay for many of your needs. As a teen, you may be responsible for luxury goods, such as music downloads and movie tickets. As an adult, you will be responsible for all of your expenses. Are you ready for more financial responsibilities? The spending secrets revealed here will prepare you.

Successful spending is about affording your expenses, finding ways to save money, and understanding the true costs of your purchases. It is also about planning. Learning to spend successfully takes time and practice. But it is worth the investment because it helps you meet your financial goals. These goals may include buying clothes for the prom, donating to a favorite charity, or contributing to your college tuition fund.

Affording your goals improves your quality of life. For example, investing in a college education can result in better job opportunities. Attending the prom can enhance your social life. In an ideal world, you could afford all the goods and services that you desire. But in the real world, your resources are limited. Your spending decisions determine how you allocate your money among such items.

Being a successful spender has other benefits besides reaching your money goals. It leads to a better awareness of the marketplace. Successful spenders must be knowledgeable about products, stores, prices, and taxes. It often makes goods and services more affordable. And it boosts confidence because wise consumers are able to spend within their means and achieve financial independence.

Should you buy a product just because it is on sale? Is a low price enough to convince you to spend your last dollar? Would you borrow money without a repayment plan? Do you know how much money you really spend? Read on to find the answers to these questions and learn the secrets of successful spending.

Don't Spend It All

Successful spending means knowing the value of your money. Think about the goods and services that you buy, such as clothes, food, or video games. Are these examples of products that you will buy only once? No, there are always different clothing fads, more meals to eat, and new video games. If you are not careful, you could easily spend all of your money and end up in debt.

Say "No" to Buying Pressures

Avoiding overspending is about resisting the buying motivators around you. For example, suppose you are at the mall with your friends. You feel pressured into buying a new pair of jeans because everyone else is doing it. Later, one of your friends also pressures you into buying expensive brand-name shoes. Your peers influenced these spending decisions. Teens like to shop in groups, and they have similar lifestyles. But your amount of spending money may

Peer pressure can lead to overspending. Stick to your budget.

differ from your friends'. When shopping with others, don't cave in to peer pressure.

Companies also pressure you into spending money. Teens have a great deal of consumer power. According to SmartMoney.com, American teenagers represent a $200 billion buying market yearly. Companies earn more money when teens buy more of their products. Businesses use tools, like ads, to encourage more consumption. Ads appear on the Internet, on television, in magazines, in newspapers, and on the radio. As with friends, do not let ads pressure you into buying goods and services. Make your own money decisions.

Think Before You Spend

Financial control is about reducing your habitual purchases, too. For example, some people regularly buy coffee on the way to school or work. Others routinely go out for lunch. A cup of coffee or a burger costs a few dollars each day. But spending a few dollars every day can add up to $50 to $100 per month, or $600 to $1,200 per year. Are there goods and services that you routinely buy? Add up how much you spend on these purchases each week and each month. Enjoying store-bought coffee and burgers less often, such as only twice a week, will decrease your chances of overspending.

Overspending is also more likely when you buy without considering both the monetary and nonmonetary costs of a purchase. For example, spending $2 on a game app has a monetary cost of $2. It also means having $2 less to buy other things, such as food or a movie download. Had you spent the $2 on food or a movie instead, you would have gained other benefits, too, like hanging out with your friends

Fascinating Financial Fact

According to the Charles Schwab 2011 Teens & Money Survey findings, 59 percent of sixteen- to eighteen-year-olds agreed with the following statement: "It's easy to get carried away and spend too much when times are good." Beware of overspending—it is easy to do!

at a restaurant or enjoying a new movie. These lost benefits are your trade-offs. When making a purchase, weigh the costs and benefits of each decision.

Remember that having money in your wallet or in the bank does not mean that you have to spend it. You have three options for your money: spend, save, or share. You already know about spending money, or buying goods and services. Saving your money is more than simply not spending it. It means putting your money away for later use. Sharing is about helping others—for example, donating money to charities.

According to the U.S. Department of Labor, 80 percent of teens have part-time jobs during the school year. Whether your income comes from working, allowances, or birthday gifts, your money is limited. Each day, you make choices about how to use these limited resources. Begin by avoiding buying motivators, reducing habitual purchases, and assessing the true costs and benefits of your purchases in order to decrease your chances of overspending.

Be Happy

Gretchen Rubin, author of *Happier at Home* and *The Happiness Project*, noted nine tips to avoid overspending on her blog. She suggested shopping quickly: the more time you spend in a store, the greater your chances of spending money. Rubin also suggested avoiding checkout line items, unnecessary upgrades, and shopping when hungry or in a rush. Think about it. If you are hungry while grocery shopping, you are more likely to overspend on food. You may even be tempted to open a package of your favorite chips and start eating in the store! Likewise, when you are in a hurry, you are more inclined to buy something without thinking or researching less-expensive options.

If you spend within your means, buying only what you can afford, you may be a happier person. You can enjoy goods and services without worrying about the bills. To avoid overspending, think about whether you can afford an item. Next, examine the benefits of making the purchase. Is it worth it? How long will it take to earn back the cost of the item? Let's say you earn $7.25 per hour. If an iPod Touch costs $300, it would take nearly forty-two hours to earn the money back for this purchase. Finally, what are you giving up by making the purchase? For example, suppose you spent $10 on lunch at a diner. You could have used this $10 for a number of song downloads instead.

Decide Whether You Need It

Many teens use the phrase "I need" when they really mean "I want." Successful spending means knowing the difference between needs and wants. Needs are items required for survival, like food, water, and shelter. These things differ from the goods and services that many teens want, such as cell phones, concert tickets, and brand-name shoes. Today, there are people in your life, such as parents or grandparents, who pay for many needs. But one day you will be responsible for the costs of these items. Developing good spending habits today will help you foot more of the bill later.

Knowing the Difference

Some goods and services are both needs and wants. For example, a teen needs clothing. But a teen may want the most expensive brand-name jacket or ten pairs of jeans. Clothing is a need, but how teens choose to spend their money can turn items into wants. Transportation is another

Fascinating Financial Fact

In 2007, the United States entered one of the worst recessions in American history. Economic growth stopped, companies closed, and people lost their jobs. In 2011, Charles Schwab reported that 58 percent of teens were still "less likely to ask for things they want[ed]."

example. Teens may need to travel from home to school. Walking or taking the bus is an option to meet this need. But taking an expensive cab ride is a want.

Think about the goods and services that you commonly purchase. Do you need them? Are you buying to meet your needs or your wants? For example, suppose that you need a pair of shoes for school. You have a choice between sneakers and a fancy pair of boots. Sneakers can be worn throughout the year and meet the requirement for gym class. The boots can be worn only in the winter. They are fashionable but not that warm or waterproof. In this case, the sneakers are a need, and the boots are a want. Which should you buy?

You should buy the sneakers because successful spending means meeting your needs first. Then you can determine the affordability of your wants. After carefully assessing your budget options, you may discover that you can buy the boots, too. Or you may pass on the boots and choose another option for your money, like saving it, giving it to charity, or making a different purchase.

Remember that growing older means paying for more of your needs. Think about some of the goods and services that

A car owner has a number of regular expenses, including insurance payments and gas.

you may pay for as an adult. First, you will need a place to live. Buying a residence comes with payments for a mortgage, homeowner's insurance, and taxes. Renting a place involves paying the rent and maintenance fees. In both cases, there are heat, electric, gas, repairs, telephone, and cable expenses to consider.

Will you own a car in your lifetime? If so, you will have to pay automobile loan and insurance payments, registration and license fees, maintenance expenses, fuel bills, and commuter costs, such as tolls and parking fees. Living expenses also include food, clothing, health costs (such as medical insurance), entertainment, and more. Spending minimal amounts on your wants today will prepare you for the future in two ways. First, it will increase your chances of living within your means. Second, saving money today means you will have more for tomorrow's expenses.

It Depends

Individual circumstances and economic conditions affect how much money is spent on wants. Suppose the economy is growing and people are earning more money. They are more likely to buy more of the goods and services that they want because they can afford them. Now, imagine that the economy is not growing and people are losing their jobs. People are less likely to be able to afford their wants. The amount of money that you spend on your wants depends on different factors, even the time of year. For example, people spend more money on wants during the holidays.

The book *10,001 Ways to Live Large on a Small Budget* recommends this advice: "Stop for ten seconds and ask yourself if this is really something you want to spend your money on. Do you really need it?" Keep in mind this ten-second rule before making a purchase. Many times, shoppers believe that they need items. But after thinking about it, they realize that the items are wants. Know the difference between your needs and wants. Your money goals should include having enough money to afford your needs. Buying most of your wants is optional.

Know the Price

Buying goods and services means paying the price. But what is the true monetary price of a good or service? When a price tag reads $5, this is not necessarily the price that you pay at the register. If you had exactly $5 in your pocket, there's a good chance that you could not afford the item. Be aware of the out-of-pocket money that you actually spend. Successful spending involves knowing the whole price.

Taxes

Many goods and services include a sales tax. This tax is money the government charges on purchased goods and services, including a variety of retail products and some foods. Tax rates depend on location. Most states in the country have state sales taxes, except Alaska, Delaware, Montana, New Hampshire, and Oregon. Some local governments charge sales taxes as well.

Each state charges sales taxes on different goods and services, such as furniture, toys, electronics, and clothing. Since taxes are calculated as a percentage of an item's price, you pay higher sales taxes on more expensive items. For example, suppose that you wanted to buy a $5 item in New Jersey, which charges a state sales tax of 7 percent. You would pay thirty-five cents in New Jersey sales taxes. If you wanted to buy a $50 item in New Jersey, the sales tax would be $3.50.

Tips and Delivery Charges

Tips and delivery charges also increase the prices of goods and services. A tip, or gratuity, is extra money the customer gives for a service, such as table service at a sit-down restaurant. Tips usually range from 15 to 20 percent of the bill. Suppose the food bill is $30. A 20 percent tip for the waiter or waitress adds an extra $6 to the bill, not including tax. Common services that require tipping include taxi rides, haircuts, and take-out food delivery. Some businesses also have tip jars for gratuities.

Shipping and handling charges are extra fees paid for delivering goods to your home. Weight, location, and delivery time affect these costs. For example, heavier items cost more to ship. Shipped items can also have surcharges, such as delivery confirmation fees. When ordering online, factor all shipping and handling charges into the product's price. Often you can find free shipping coupons online. Take a look!

Maintenance and Accessories

Maintenance and accessory fees accompany many goods and services. For example, buying a cell phone is not a onetime cost. There are monthly bills to pay or minutes to

Fascinating Financial Fact

The government can use taxes to influence your spending decisions. In 2012, thirty states charged sales tax on soda. Several cities also considered higher taxes and bans on sugar-sweetened drinks to deter people from buying them.

purchase. Monthly charges can easily cost between $50 and $150. Cell phones also have maintenance contracts and accessories that increase their costs. Some of these fees, such as warranty contracts for fixing or replacing a phone, are paid at the time of the phone purchase. Accessories and extra services from phone covers to ringtones also add up. And beware of termination fees for canceling your phone service earlier than the contract end date.

Many other goods and services, such as cars and bikes, also have maintenance and accessory fees. Car maintenance requires gas fill-ups, oil changes, and repairs. Bike accessories include helmets, lights, and pumps. Some electronics require chargers, headsets, and protective covers. Think about the goods and services that you use each day. How many of these items come with extra costs? Be aware that many goods and services involve ongoing costs.

Making a purchase often involves more than just the price tag. It can include taxes, tips, shipping and handling, maintenance, and accessory charges. Make sure to include these fees in the product's price. Factor the real price into

Budget for unexpected expenses, such as car repairs.

your budget. Do you have enough spending money to cover a product's price with tax? Is it worth spending money on shipping and handling if you can buy the same product locally? Do you need a warranty contract or accessories? Can you afford to buy a product with monthly charges? Successful spending means knowing the whole price so that you can accurately assess affordability.

Get the Most Bang for Your Buck

Successful spending means knowing that vendors charge different prices for comparable goods and services. One store may price a loaf of bread at $2.50, while another may charge $3.75 for the same loaf of bread. Why spend an extra $1.25 to buy the same loaf? Successful spending means getting the most for your money. This goal can be achieved with a tool called comparative shopping.

Comparative Shopping

Comparative shopping involves comparing the prices of goods and services from different vendors. To shop in this way, follow these steps:

1. Visit stores or online vendors that offer the same or similar products.

2. Take notes in a price book. This book should be portable, like a small notebook or a saved document on a mobile device. A price book records the store name, product name, brand name (such as Coke or Pepsi), and product price.
3. Compare the prices for the same product at different stores. Also compare the prices for different brands of a product within the same store. Store brands are generally the least expensive.
4. Circle or highlight the stores, brands, and sites that offer consistently lower prices. Take note of the lowest price that you found for each product.

A price book is especially helpful for goods you buy often, such as foods that you eat regularly or personal care products (shampoo, soap, etc.) that you use again and again.

Use Electronics

The Web can help with comparative shopping. Some sites provide price comparisons for different products, such as video games, computers, clothing, furniture, health and beauty items, and jewelry. Other sites compare one type of product. For example, GasBuddy.com reports the lowest gas prices in an area by comparing nearby stations. Expedia, Priceline, Travelocity, Orbitz, and Hotwire provide price comparisons for travel. According to an article on eBizMBA.com, the most popular price-comparison sites in 2012 were Bizrate.com, Nextag.com, ShopLocal.com, Slickdeals.net, and Woot.com.

Apps help buyers locate the lowest prices. Let your smartphone do the shopping!

Apps also aid customers in finding the lowest prices for goods and services. Price Check by Amazon, RedLaser, ShopSavvy, Pic2shop, Goodzer, PriceGrabber, and SnapTell are free comparative shopping apps. Shoppers need to check the compatibility of the apps with their smartphones and other mobile devices. Just compare prices by scanning the product's bar code, taking the product's picture, or speaking the product's

Fascinating Financial Fact

According to ProfitFuzion.com, 51 percent of mobile comparison shoppers are between ages eighteen and thirty-nine.

name. Some apps provide product reviews in addition to price comparisons from various Web sites.

Your Lowest Price

Now suppose that you found the lowest price for a video game. Does a successful spender always buy the game at that price? No. Successful spending is also about knowing what price you are willing to pay. Consider another example, such as wanting a new pair of boots. In your budget, you list "boots" as a short-term goal, or a financial goal that you hope to achieve in less than six months. You use comparative shopping to find the lowest price for your choice of boots. Your budget allows $50 to purchase this good. But the lowest price that you found was $75.

Do you buy the boots? Spending wisely is about following your budget. Your spending limit for new boots is $50. Even at the lowest price, you still cannot afford the boots. Do not feel pressured into buying goods and services just because they may have relatively low prices. You still need to be able to afford those prices. Comparative shopping helps you find competitive prices. Then you can make a spending decision. Comparative shopping takes time and effort. But with this tool, you are on your way to spending successfully.

MYTHS
AND
FACTS

FACT

Myth
Goods and services cost the same in every store and on every Web site.

Businesses can charge different prices for comparable or identical goods and services.

FACT

Myth
Consumers should always buy products that are offered at the lowest prices or they are missing a great deal.

Even at the lowest prices, consumers may be unable to afford the products and should not buy them.

FACT

Myth
All consumer expenditures are planned purchases.

Many people are impulse shoppers. They spontaneously buy goods and services without considering the financial consequences. Retailers are aware of this and often set up displays at strategic locations, such as near the checkout, to tempt consumers to make unplanned purchases.

Track It

Successful spending requires awareness of your spending habits. How much do you spend on goods and services each week? If you track your expenditures, you'll find out. Tracking also reveals your buying preferences and the actual costs of your purchases. Before you begin tracking your spending, guess how much money you spend each week. After you complete your tracking spreadsheet, compare your guess with the real amount. Will the two numbers match? Probably not!

Making the Spreadsheet

A spreadsheet is a way of displaying data using rows and columns. Popular computer spreadsheet programs include Microsoft Excel, OpenOffice, and Lotus 1-2-3. These programs provide tables for you to fill in. Check your home, school, or library computers to find out about their spreadsheet programs. Using this software, you can make and save your own tracking document. If you need help, ask someone or check out online spreadsheet tutorials. Most high schools offer computer courses that include lessons on creating spreadsheets. For a class assignment, try tracking your expenses.

You can also create your own spreadsheet using grid paper or a notebook. Whether using a computer or a pencil, create a spreadsheet with three columns and at least ten rows. Label the columns "Purchase," "Cost," and "Notes." In the "Purchase" column, record the good or service you bought. In the "Cost" column, input the full dollar amount of the purchase (including taxes, tips, and other charges). Use the "Notes" column for things that you want to remember about a purchase. For example, suppose that you bought a birthday gift. It is helpful to remember that this was a onetime purchase and not a regular expense.

Successfully tracking spending depends on recording each purchase and its correct dollar amount. What is the best way to ensure that you have accurately recorded these items? Keep your receipts. Each time that you make a purchase, you receive a receipt that records your purchase and

Fascinating Financial Fact

Teens prefer to shop at brick-and-mortar stores. Teenagers find online shopping difficult because most don't own credit cards or want their parents to have to sign off on all purchases that use online payment services, like PayPal.

its dollar amount. You can use these receipts to fill in the spreadsheet. For example, suppose that you went to a restaurant and received a receipt for $10. Your spreadsheet entry may read, "Purchase: Restaurant meal; Cost: $10; Note: Ate at Burger Nosh." After one week of recording your expenses, analyze the information.

Analyze It

Begin by looking at the purchases listed on the spreadsheet and grouping your expenses into categories. Then find a sum for each category. For example, add up all the expenses in the "Eating Out" category. Make another table with two columns, "Expense" and "Weekly Total." List each category, like "Eating Out," in the "Expense" column. Record the sums for each category, and place them in the "Weekly Total" column. To find out how much you probably spend in

EXPENSES

MORTGAGE / RENT

UTILITIES

Gas / Oil

Electricity

Water / Sewer

Telephone

Cable TV

FOOD / GROCERY

Put your expenses into categories and add up the totals. Find out how much you really spend.

each category in a month, multiply your weekly total by 4.3. That is your monthly total. To find out how much you would likely spend in a year, multiply your monthly total by twelve.

This spreadsheet provides successful spenders with a lot of information. It allows them to identify where most of their money is being spent. Look at your spreadsheet. Which goods and services do you spend the most money on? Circle your top three expenses. The spreadsheet also reveals consumer preferences, or the goods and services that buyers prefer to buy. For example, consumers discover which stores or restaurants they frequent most. You may even discover that you already bought too much of a certain good, even though you thought you "needed" more!

Once you have this data, you can start to exercise more control over your spending by setting a budget. According to an article on Investopedia.com, assigning a percentage to each expense category may be more useful than a dollar amount. For example, you may decide to allocate 20 percent of your budget for food or 10 percent for clothing. Remember that as your life circumstances change, so do your budget percentages. For instance, moving into your own place means adding a housing percentage to your budget. In the next section, you will learn how knowledge of your expenses helps you lower your spending, balance your budget, and achieve your money goals.

Make a Budget

Successful spending is living within a realistic budget. A budget is a financial plan that helps you achieve your money goals. It lists income, expenses, and both short-term and long-term financial goals. Income is money earned from working or allowances. It can also include other sources, such birthday and holiday gifts. An expense is money that is spent. Income goes into your bank account, wallet, or other money storage; expenses go out. Spending is successful when income is greater than expenses, or at least equal to them.

Achieving Goals

What do wise spenders do with their excess income? They reach their money goals! Examples include buying a long-awaited concert ticket or a new computer, helping to pay for college, or donating to a favorite charity. All of these items cost money. The amount of money depends on the item's cost. To afford these goal items, people save money. Most financial goals require more money

Use some of your savings to achieve a long-term money goal, such as purchasing a computer.

than teens have in their wallets. Since it takes longer to save for a $500 computer than a $50 concert ticket, the computer is a long-term goal. The concert ticket is an example of a short-term goal.

Make a budget to afford your goals. Begin by creating a table with three columns and at least ten rows. Label the columns "Income," "Expenses," and "Money Goals." Under "Income," list all sources of weekly income with dollar amounts, like a $5 allowance. Don't include items that are not received weekly, such as birthday money. Under "Expenses," list the weekly expenses you already tracked in your spreadsheet. The "Money Goals" column includes both short-term and long-term goals. Popular money goals include buying clothes, electronics, and entertainment (like concert tickets).

Save It!

A budget reveals the connection between income and expenses. Is your income greater than your expenses? If it is, you are saving money! If it isn't, you are spending too much money. Where can you decrease expenses? Look at your tracking worksheet and find ways to spend less. For example, suppose you are overspending by $5 each week. Your spreadsheet reveals that you spend $20 a week (or $4 a day) to buy lunch. Bringing your own lunch from home twice a week will save you $8 and turn you into a saver.

Be realistic about your budget. Write down actual amounts for income and expenses, and choose affordable goals. Be diligent about recording these amounts. If you spend $60 on food for the month, do not write down $20. This will leave you with $40 less in your budget for expenses and goals. Making

Fascinating Financial Fact

Do today's teens save or overspend? According to the Charles Schwab 2011 Teens & Money Survey findings, teens received an average weekly income of $50 and spent an average of $18.50. So teens in 2011 were savers!

these errors frequently will soon mean that your budget no longer reflects your true financial picture. To pay expenses, save money, and meet goals, you need a realistic budget—even if it shows that you need to change your spending habits, like spending less on eating out.

You also need to stick to your budget. Suppose you want to save $75 each month toward your financial goals. Your income is $200, so you can spend and donate $125 at the most. At first, you spend $200 or more each month. You don't have any money left over for your goals. In fact, you end up in debt (owing money). What happened? You did not follow

Look for ways to enjoy goods and services without spending money, such as using the library.

your budget. You spent more than your income, without saving for your goals. After you repay your debts, you decide to follow your budget. During each of the next six months, you spend and donate less than $125. Soon you have enough money to afford your short-term goals. By following your budget, you spent within your means and met some of your financial goals.

Remember to update your budget. Incomes can change. For example, your allowance may increase, or you may decide to work fewer hours. Expenses also change due to changes in buying preferences or prices. And money goals change as you afford old goals and make new ones. Reevaluate your budget regularly to ensure that it still reflects your current income, expenses, and goals.

It's Not All About the Money

Sometimes it is difficult to resist the urge to spend or donate more than your budget allows. In these cases, get creative. For example, suppose a natural disaster occurs, and you want to give a donation to help others. Also, imagine that you are not a great saver. In fact, your expenses equal your income most months. Not to worry! You can help in nonmonetary ways, like volunteering your time.

Other goods and services also have nonmonetary alternatives. For example, consider borrowing books and DVDs from the library, rather than buying them. You can also barter, or trade, your skills or items for something else. Suppose your friend wants someone to help her paint, and you want a ride to the concert. You could paint in exchange for the ride. She saves on hiring a painter, and you save on gas.

10 GREAT QUESTIONS
to Ask a Financial Expert

1. How can I decrease my spending?

2. Can fewer expenses and more income help me reach my money goals?

3. Do people spend more money on their needs or wants?

4. What are the needs that I will be financially responsible for as an adult?

5. How can I identify and stop habitual spending and impulse spending?

6. How can shopping tools, like coupons and rebates, result in more successful spending?

7. Do most wise spenders use rewards programs?

8. How can I stay out of debt?

9. Do wise spenders ever borrow money to pay for their expenses?

10. How could the country's economic performance affect my budget?

Do the Research

Successful spending means researching products to pay less for them. As discussed, keeping a price book allows shoppers to keep track of prices for regularly used goods and services. Then shoppers can determine the lowest prices for comparable products and save money when they spend.

As shoppers record prices, they may notice that store brands are generally less expensive than other brand names. A store-brand product is a good that is manufactured by the store's corporation. For example, the popular Florida grocery-store chain Publix sells Publix yogurt and Publix bread. Such products usually cost less than other brand-name yogurts and breads.

Coupons and Rebates

Coupons also help save money. A coupon is a voucher that allows buyers to receive a certain percentage off the price, known as a discount. Coupons are found online, in the mail, in newspapers, or in stores. To find a coupon online, input the product or store with the word "coupon." For example, suppose a shopper wants to search for a coupon for the Gap store. He or she would

Certain Web sites help buyers save money and discover new goods and services.

type the words "Gap coupon" into a search engine, such as Yahoo! or Google. Then the shopper could choose between printable coupons for store purchases or codes for online orders. Online shoppers can often find coupons for free shipping and even free returns.

There are also apps to help shoppers find the best prices for goods and services at nearby retailers. For example, the Coupons app and FourSquare app provide coupons for nearby stores, restaurants, and movie theaters. The Cellfire app even sends coupon reminders as shoppers enter specific stores.

Can coupons really save you money? According to the Promotion Marketing Association Educational Foundation, which hosts National Coupon Month, consumers saved $2 billion in the first six months of 2011. Using coupons to pay lower prices for goods and services helps you become a successful spender.

Also, be on the lookout for products with rebates. A rebate is a partial refund on a specific product. For example, some cell phone companies offer rebates on their phones. This means that a shopper pays a phone's price and then receives some of this money back, such as $50. Billions of dollars in rebates are offered each year, and up to 60 percent go unredeemed. However, beware of rebate scams, which can be researched online at the Federal Trade Commission's Web site (http://www.ftc.gov) and other sites.

Less Expensive Alternatives

Other ways to pay lower prices for goods and services include garage sales, online auctions, and thrift stores. Garage sales offer many used goods at discounted prices. You may spot a garage sale while driving or see one advertised on a flyer. You can also research garage sales in your area at Web sites such as YardSaleSearch.com or GarageSaleFinder.com. Other sites, such as eBay, offer used goods for sale on the Web. eBay is an example of an online auction house, where sellers and buyers use bidding to make price decisions. Thrift stores are also sources of less expensive used goods. Goodwill, for example is an organization that collects donated goods and offers them for sale in its nationwide thrift stores.

Teens can pay bargain prices for clothes, shoes, purses, and other goods at thrift stores.

Think about making your own goods or providing your own services. For example, suppose your school is hosting a bake sale, and students are asked to bring in cakes. How can you afford this donation? Rather than buy a cake, make your own by using the ingredients that you already have in your kitchen. Other things that you can do yourself include beauty care (do your own nails, for example), make your own lunch, and wash your own car.

Stay Informed

Informed consumers make wise spenders. Read reviews of potential purchases, particularly long-term goal items. Sites such as ConsumerReports.org and CNET.com provide rankings, pros, cons, and ratings for various products. For example, you can look up a specific cell phone and learn about its features (such as a camera, Bluetooth capability, and touchscreen),

Fascinating Financial Fact

Some coupon sites, such as Coupons.com, SmartSource.com, and RetailMeNot.com, provide coupons for various products and stores. They have different daily, weekly, or monthly specials. Other coupon sites, such as Groupon and LivingSocial, send e-mails with special deals in certain locations.

manufacturing company (such as Samsung), ratings, and price ranges. ConsumersReports.org also provides user reviews, complete with star ratings and bottom lines.

Organizations such as the Better Business Bureau (BBB) disclose consumer complaints on certain products and report on misleading advertising and selling practices. You can file a complaint about a product with this organization by completing a six-step online application. The Better Business Bureau gives accreditation to companies that meet certain standards, such as satisfactorily handling consumer complaints. Companies pay a fee that includes accreditation monitoring.

Beware! Just because some products are less expensive than others does not mean they are the best deals. For example, suppose you buy the cheapest cell phone in the store. Soon you discover that it has poor reception and breaks easily. This cell phone was not a wise purchase. Now suppose you read reviews of different cell phones. Then you buy a good-quality phone that cost $50 more than the cheapest phone in the store. This was a smarter shopping decision.

Avoid Impulse Shopping

Wise spending is about saying "no" to impulse shopping. Impulse shopping is buying without having planned to make a purchase—for example, spontaneously buying candy or a magazine at the checkout counter. These purchases may give shoppers a powerful lift, as they suddenly buy something just because they feel like it. Other times, impulse spending may be caused by peer pressure. According to C&E Vision's industry blog, 40 percent of consumer spending is impulse buying. Impulse purchases accounted for $4.2 trillion in spending the last three months of 2010 alone.

The Culprit: Sales

The C&E Vision blog reported that the biggest motivation for impulse buying is a sale. Items on sale cost less than their regular prices. Often when shoppers see sale items, they buy. Shoppers may even convince themselves that they "need" products or that the deals are too good to pass up. Are sales bad? No. If you have properly budgeted for a good or service that is on sale, you are being a smart shopper to buy it at a lower price. But if you buy an item only because it is on sale, you're being an impulse shopper. You have not considered if you need the good or can afford it.

Suppose you are at the mall with friends. Your best friend buys a new sweater and wants you to buy one, too. She even points out that the sweater is on sale. The sweater is 50 percent off, and it would look great on you. Your friend keeps pressuring you to make the purchase. As a wise spender,

Many consumers buy unnecessary goods and services simply because they are on sale. Think before you spend.

what should you do? First, consider your budget. Can you afford this extra expense? Next, think about the trade-offs. If you buy the sweater, what other future purchases will you have to give up? Will this purchase delay attaining your financial goals? Spending wisely means not impulsively making purchases because of factors like sales or peer pressure. Spending wisely means taking the time to stop and think about your financial decisions.

Stop It

Impulse shoppers face real consequences, like overspending. Impulse shopping can quickly add up and cause teens to owe more money than they earn. Often impulse shoppers don't realize how much they have spent until they don't have enough money to pay the bills or enough cash left for ATM withdrawals. Many impulse shoppers feel guilty when they discover the amount they spent and are hard-pressed to find ways to pay for their expenses. Sometimes buyer's remorse results in returning the items they impulsively bought. But some sale items are final-sale merchandise and cannot be returned.

Fascinating Financial Fact

Shopping can be addictive. According to a 2006 Stanford University study published in the *American Journal of Psychiatry*, seventeen million Americans are compulsive shoppers, and almost half are men.

How can you avoid impulse shopping? The ten-second rule is a good place to start. But waiting two days before buying a good or service that costs more than $25 is even better. Making a shopping list and sticking to it also reduces temptation. For example, buy only food that appears on the grocery list. Suppose you need shoes. At the mall, stick to buying shoes, even if the clothes and electronics on sale are calling your name. Before you pay at the register, check your cart. Do you have only the items on your list? If you have extra goods, put them back! You can always add these items to your money goals.

Don't be afraid to walk away from a purchase. Many salespeople can make consumers feel that they have to buy an item right away. They may claim that an item is on sale for only another twenty-four hours or that there is only one product left in stock. These tactics can intimidate buyers and pressure them into impulse spending. Remember to wait before you buy. Ask yourself if you need or want the product and if it is in your budget. Chances are you will find a comparable product at a good price when you are ready and able to buy it. Likewise, products that have limited stock in one store can often be found in other stores or online. Think before you buy to avoid the pitfalls of impulse spending.

Earn While You Spend

Wise spenders earn rewards for shopping. While spending money within their budgets, these shoppers gain benefits such as goods, services, discounts on future purchases, and even cash. Can you imagine being rewarded for buying goods and services? Companies have rewards programs to encourage customer loyalty. They want to ensure that consumers like you continue to buy their products.

Loyalty Programs

Many teens frequent coffee shops, restaurants, game shops, and clothing stores that offer loyalty programs. For example, Starbucks Rewards provides loyal customers with free drinks, refills, syrups, soy milk, birthday beverages, and personalized coupons. Dunkin' Donuts' DD Perks Rewards program also offers regular customers rewards, including Dunkin' Dollars that can be redeemed for store items. Some programs require customers to register their rewards cards online, and some cards work like debit cards. They allow a specific

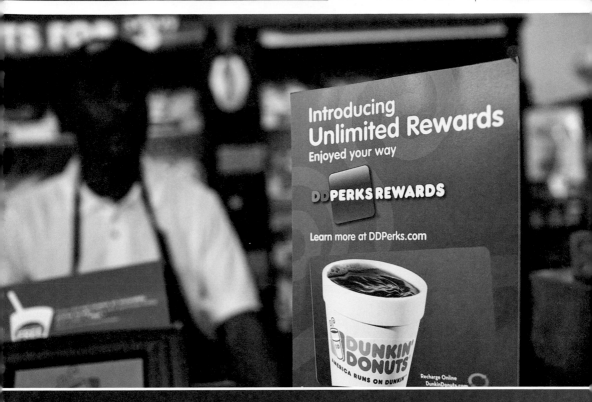

Save money by signing up for loyalty programs at your favorite stores.

amount of money to be withdrawn for purchases. For example, $10 on a Starbucks Rewards card is like having $10 in cash to spend only at Starbucks.

Teens can also take advantage of rewards programs from GameStop, jcpenney, Kmart, Gap, Old Navy, H&M, and American Eagle Outfitters. The rewards programs are a win-win for stores and successful spenders. For the stores, they increase sales volume, which allows businesses to earn more money. For customers, they earn points, which are traded for benefits. For example, GameStop's PowerUp Rewards allows customers to earn points for buying merchandise. These points can then be traded in for gaming gear, discounts, collectibles, and coupons.

Fascinating Financial Fact

According to SmartMoney.com, the average American household participates in eighteen different consumer rewards programs. However, only 17 percent of Americans reported that loyalty programs are "very influential" in where they decide to spend, according to the 2011 COLLOQUY Cross-Cultural Loyalty Study.

Online Rewards

Shoppers can receive rewards for purchasing goods and services online. With some programs, consumers receive actual cash back to make other purchases. One popular cash-back shopping site, Ebates.com, gives you bucks just for spending. Ebates has more than 1,200 stores on its site for shopping, from the Apple Store to Walgreens. Becoming a member requires an e-mail address and password of your choice. Ebates also offers coupons for in-store shopping at a limited number of stores. As of 2012, Ebates members had earned more than $100 million cash back.

Other rewards programs are point-based. This means that you earn points for shopping via specific sites, such as MyPoints.com, that link to a variety of retailers. Then you can trade these points for rewards, including gifts cards for stores and restaurants, travel cards, and cash payments to a PayPal account or Visa prepaid card. Whether you are choosing a cash-back or point rewards system, beware of scams. Don't sign up for programs that require fees. MyPoints.com,

Ebates.com, and other reputable sites are free. Also, read the terms and conditions carefully before agreeing to them.

Get Others Involved

Ask your parent if he or she has a grocery store card or credit card that yields rewards. Turn your whole family into successful spenders. Grocery store rewards cards can offer discounts on goods and services, money off the total bill, and even free goods (such as a free turkey at Thanksgiving). Many credit card companies offer a variety of perks. For example, the Merrill Lynch Visa credit card provides customers with rewards such as travel points, goods, and gift cards that can be used for the Merrill Lynch college savings plan or to pay off purchases. Your school can also earn points in rewards programs, such as the TI Technology Rewards Program by Texas Instruments (TI). This program allows teachers to exchange points from student calculator purchases for TI goods and services.

Look at your tracking spreadsheet. Are there stores where you frequently shop? Use a search engine to find out if these businesses have rewards programs or ask a cashier at the store. Some programs provide a punch card to carry in your wallet, with promises such as, "Indulge in any ten delicious drinks from the coffee bar and get one free." Signing up for customer loyalty programs earns you rewards, and it's often free. But be careful. Just as with sales and other buying incentives, be sure that you are sticking to your budget. Do not feel pressured into spending more money just because you want to earn more benefits.

Try Not to Borrow

Wise spending means not borrowing money to pay for your regular purchases. When people's expenses are greater than their income, they often borrow money to pay bills. This creates debt, or money owed. Debt has to be repaid. If people take out loans, they have to repay the amount owed plus the cost of borrowing, known as interest. Debt is very costly. Some teens borrow money from relatives or friends. Often these people do not charge interest. But teens are still obligated to repay their financial debts.

Be Careful—It Adds Up!

Successful spenders do not spend more than they earn. Think about your budget. If you spend the same amount as you earn, you have a balanced budget. You are not in debt, but you also don't have any extra money to afford your financial goals. If you spend more than you earn, you are overspending and will likely incur debt in order to pay your bills. This can begin a dangerous cycle of overspending, borrowing money, and being unable to repay the borrowed money. Even if you

Don't fall into the trap of using too many credit cards and being unable to pay off the balances.

decrease your expenditures, you may be unable to save enough money to repay your debt.

Debt can create a vicious cycle, particularly with credit cards. A credit card is a way to borrow money. Cardholders must repay their expenses or they incur fees for unpaid balances. For example, suppose a person uses his or her credit card to purchase $500 worth of goods. When the credit card bill arrives, he or she repays $200 and incurs interest charges of $70 for being unable to repay the $300. Now the credit card spender owes $370. Over the next few months, this cycle continues. Soon the credit card spender cannot even repay the interest fees and still owes the original balance. According to an article in *Forbes*, the average credit card debt for all American households was $6,722 in March 2012.

Fascinating Financial Fact

According to *U.S. News & World Report*, student loan balances in the third quarter of 2011 were $870 billion—even higher than the outstanding credit card balances in the United States!

Spend What You Can Afford

How can you avoid debt, including the vicious credit card cycle? Do not spend more than you earn or have a plan to repay what you do spend. For most teens, income should be equal to or greater than their expenses. But after high school, things change. People want to afford goods and services that cost more than they have in their bank accounts, such as college tuitions, cars, and houses. These items enhance people's lives. Before borrowing money for these expenses, make plans to repay it.

For example, going to college has many benefits, such as more job opportunities and higher income potential. But college is expensive, and many students take out loans to pay for higher education. If you plan to be one of these students, figure out how you can pay back your loan over time. Will your expected future salary allow you to repay your debts and pay your other bills? If not, consider less expensive college options, like state and community colleges. The process of repaying a loan begins before you borrow money. It starts with a plan for how to repay it.

A high school senior works on obtaining college loans. Research ways to repay debts incurred by big-ticket expenses like college before borrowing money.

Borrowing money is also about reputation. Suppose a friend borrowed money from you and did not repay it. Would you want to lend money to this friend again? Probably not! Financial institutions, like banks, operate the same way. If people do not pay their bills, banks are less likely to lend them money. How do banks know if a potential borrower has paid his or her bills? They check the borrower's credit rating, which assesses a person's history of meeting financial obligations. Banks are more likely to lend money to people with good credit histories—and offer them lower interest rates. Build a good credit history, and you will have more options in the future.

Glossary

budget A financial plan that includes income, expenses, and goals for spending and saving.

comparative shopping The process of analyzing the prices of goods and services from different vendors in order to make a purchase.

coupon A voucher that yields a certain percentage off the price of a product or service.

debt Money owed to a person, financial institution, or other organization.

expense An amount spent or required to be spent on the purchase of a good or service.

habitual purchase An expense incurred on a regular basis, such as weekly.

impulse shopping The act of buying without a plan to make a purchase.

income Money earned from work, investments, property, or other sources.

money goal A financial aim that a person would like to achieve.

need A good or service required for survival, such as food, clothing, or shelter.

overspend To spend in excess of one's income, or more than one can afford.

peer pressure Influence by people of the same age or ability, such as friends or classmates.

price The amount of money for which something is purchased, sold, or offered for sale.

price book A portable record of the prices of goods and
services offered by different vendors.

rebate A partial refund on a product.

receipt A statement showing the details of a sale, including
the date, merchant name and address, the items sold
and their prices, taxes, total, and the form of payment
used.

rewards program Benefits received by customers who
frequently buy from the same vendor; also known as a
loyalty program.

sales tax Money paid to the government for the purchase
of some goods and services.

vendor Person or company that sells a good or service.

want A desired good or service that is not needed for
survival.

For More Information

Boys & Girls Clubs of America
1275 Peachtree Street NE
Atlanta, GA 30309
(404) 487-5700
Web site: http://www.bgca.org
With the support of the Charles Schwab Foundation, the Boys
   & Girls Clubs of America offers the Money Matters: Make It
   Count program to improve teens' money management
   skills. The Web site (http://moneymattersmakeitcount.com)
   of the program has helpful information, interactive activities,
   games, and tools.

Canadian Bankers Association (CBA)
Box 348, Commerce Court West
199 Bay Street, 30th Floor
Toronto, ON M5L 1G2
Canada
(416) 362-6092
Web site: http://www.cba.ca
The CBA works to promote an understanding of the banking
   industry in Canada. It provides information on banking and
   financial literacy for children, teens, and their families.

Council for Economic Education (CEE)
122 East 42nd Street, Suite 2600

New York, NY 10168
(800) 338-1192
Web site: http://www.councilforeconed.org
The Council for Economic Education focuses on the economic
    and financial education of students from kindergarten
    through high school. It offers a variety of educational
    resources for teens, parents, and educators.

Federal Deposit Insurance Corporation (FDIC)
550 17th Street NW
Washington, DC 20429-9990
(877) ASK-FDIC [275-3342]
Web site: http://www.fdic.gov
The FDIC is an independent agency that works to main-
    tain stability and public confidence in the nation's
    financial system. It provides financial education and
    literacy resources to financially empower teens and
    adults.

Financial Consumer Agency of Canada (FCAC)
427 Laurier Avenue West, 6th Floor
Ottawa, ON K1R 1B9
Canada
(866) 461-FCAC [3222]
Web site: http://www.fcac-acfc.gc.ca/eng/education
This Canadian agency has developed educational programs
    and materials to help Canadians increase their financial
    and personal money-management skills and knowledge.

U.S. Department of the Treasury
1500 Pennsylvania Avenue NW
Washington, DC 20220
(202) 622-2000
Web site: http://www.treasury.gov
The Department of the Treasury is the executive agency
    responsible for promoting economic prosperity and ensur-
    ing the financial security of the United States. Along with
    other federal entities, it provides financial education
    resources to the public through the Web site MyMoney.gov.

Web Sites

Due to the changing nature of Internet links, Rosen Publishing
has developed an online list of Web sites related to the sub-
ject of this book. This site is updated regularly. Please use
this link to access the list:

http://www.rosenlinks.com/SGFE/Spend

For Further Reading

Bloch, Phillip. *The Shopping Diet: Spend Less and Get More.* New York, NY: Gallery Books, 2010.

Butler, Tamsen. *The Complete Guide to Personal Finance: For Teenagers and College Students.* Ocala, FL: Atlantic Publishing, 2010.

Chatzky, Jean Sherman, and Erwin Haya. *Not Your Parents' Money Book: Making, Saving, and Spending Your Own Money.* New York, NY: Simon & Schuster Books for Young Readers, 2010.

Denega, Danielle. *Smart Money: How to Manage Your Cash* (Choices). New York, NY: Franklin Watts, 2008.

Don't Break the Bank: A Student's Guide to Managing Money 2012. Lawrenceville, NJ: Peterson's, 2012.

Freedman, Jeri. *Consumer Smarts: Getting the Most for Your Money* (Get Smart with Your Money). New York, NY: Rosen Publishing, 2013.

Gerber, Larry. *Top 10 Tips for Developing Money Management Skills* (Tips for Success). New York, NY: Rosen Central, 2013.

Hansen, Mark, and Kevin S. Ferber. *Success 101 for Teens: Dollars and Sense for a Winning Financial Life.* St. Paul, MN: Paragon House, 2012.

Hollander, Barbara. *Managing Money* (Life Skills). Chicago, IL: Heinemann Library, 2008.

Monteverde, Matt. *Frequently Asked Questions About Budgeting and Money Management* (FAQ: Teen Life). New York, NY: Rosen Publishing, 2009.

Peterson, Judy Monroe. *First Budget Smarts* (Get Smart with Your Money). New York, NY: Rosen Publishing, 2010.

Scheff, Anna. *Shopping Smarts: How to Choose Wisely, Find Bargains, Spot Swindles, and More.* Minneapolis, MN: Twenty-First Century Books, 2012.

Silver, Don. *High School Money Book.* Los Angeles, CA: Adams-Hall Publishing, 2008.

Vickers, Rebecca. *101 Ways to Be Smart About Money* (101 Series). Chicago, IL: Raintree, 2012.

Wood, Alice, and Glenn Rifkin. *Wealth Watchers: A Simple Program to Help You Spend Less and Save More.* New York, NY: Free Press, 2010.

Bibliography

American Psychotherapy Association. "Bought Out and $pent." Retrieved September 2012 (http://www.american psychotherapy.com/about/apa609.php).

Andriotis, Annamaria. "6 Rewards Programs Worth Your Loyalty." SmartMoney.com, March 22, 2011. Retrieved September 2012 (http://www.smartmoney.com/ spend/family-money/the-best-loyalty-programs -1300230426274).

BruceBucks.com. "Dangers of Impulse Buying." November 1, 2010. Retrieved September 2012 (http://www.bruce bucks.com/2010/11/dangers -of-impulse-buying).

C&E Vision's Industry News Feed. "The Truth About Impulse Buying." March 14, 2011. Retrieved September 2012 (http://blog.eyesurf.info/?p=2727).

Charles Schwab & Co., Inc. "2011 Teens & Money Survey Findings: Insights into Money Attitudes, Behaviors, and Expectations of 16- to 18-Year-Olds." Retrieved September 2012 (http://www.aboutschwab.com/ images/press/teensmoneyfactsheet.pdf).

Chen, Tim. "Bad News: Credit Card Debt Is Down." Forbes. com, May 30, 2012. Retrieved September 2012 (http:// www.forbes.com/sites/moneybuilder/2012/05/30/ bad-news-credit-card-debt-is-down).

ConsumerReports.org. "Shop Smart with Mobile Apps."
December 2011. Retrieved September 2012 (http://www
.consumerreports.org).

eBizMBA.com. "Top 15 Most Popular Comparison Shopping
Websites." October 2012. Retrieved October 2012 (http://
www.ebizmba.com/articles/shopping-websites).

Fottrell, Quentin. "Why Teens Snub Online Retail." SmartMoney
.com, July 26, 2012. Retrieved September 2012 (http://
blogs.smartmoney.com/advice/2012/07/26/
why-teens-snub-online-retail).

Hamm, Trent. *365 Ways to Live Cheap: Your Everyday
Guide to Saving Money.* Avon, MA: Adams Media, 2008.

Hlavinka, Kelly, and Jim Sullivan. "The Rules of Engagement:
Loyalty in the U.S. and Canada." *COLLOQUYtalk*,
December 2011. Retrieved September 2012 (http://
www.marketingpower.com/ResourceLibrary/Documents/
Content%20Partner%20Documents/COLLOQUY/2012/
loyalty_us_canada.pdf).

Ingram, Leah. *Suddenly Frugal: How to Live Happier &
Healthier for Less.* Avon, MA: Adams Media, 2010.

Knowledge@Wharton. "The Soda Tax Gamble: Will It Really
Make Us Healthier?" September 12, 2012. Retrieved
December 2012 (http://knowledge.wharton.upenn.edu).

Kurtzleben, Danielle. "5 Shocking Facts About Student
Loan Debt." *U.S. News and World Report*, March 6,
2012. Retrieved September 2012 (http://www.usnews
.com/news/articles/2012/03/06/5-shocking-facts
-about-student-loan-debt).

Loo, Tristan. "Mobile Comparison Shopping Statistics."
ProfitFuzion.com. Retrieved September 2012 (http://www
.profitfuzion.com/marketing-articles/mobile-comparison-
shopping-statistics.html).

Marquit, Miranda. "Top 10 Best (and Free) Online Budget
Tools." GoodFinancialCents.com, December 22, 2011.
Retrieved September 2012 (http://www.goodfinancial
cents.com/best-free-online-budgeting-tools).

Mathias, Shari. "Online Shopping Rewards Programs." Yahoo!
Voices, December 2, 2009. Retrieved October 2012
(http://voices.yahoo.com/online-shopping-rewards-pro-
grams-4989706.html).

Montaldo, Donna L. "Taking Control of Rebates: Just Say No to
Not Getting Your Rebate Check." About.com. Retrieved
September 2012 (http://couponing.about.com/od/
bargainshoppingtips/a/rebatefraud.htm).

Murray, Katherine. "Five Free Comparison-Shopping
Smartphone Apps." *TechRepublic*, December 5, 2011.
Retrieved September 2012 (http://www.techrepublic.com/
blocg/five-apps/
five-free-comparison-shopping-smartphone-apps/1181).

Rubin, Gretchen. "Money: 9 Tips to Avoid Overspending."
The Happiness Project, February 4, 2009. Retrieved
October 2012 (http://happiness-project.com/
happiness_project/2009/02/money-9-tips-to-avoid
-overspending).

Simpson, Stephen D. "Custom Budgeting for Young Adults."
Investopedia.com, June 2, 2010. Retrieved October

2012 (http://www.investopedia.com/financial-edge/
0610/custom-budgeting-for-young-adults.aspx
#axzz2LMQLJXKA).

10,001 Ways to Live Large on a Small Budget. New York,
NY: Skyhorse Publishing, 2009.

Texas Instruments, Inc. "TI Technology Rewards Program—
About the Program." Retrieved September 2012
(http://education.ti.com/educationportal/sites/US/
nonProductMulti/support_VPP.html).

Index

About the Author

Barbara Gottfried Hollander has authored several economics and business books, including *Money Matters: An Introduction to Economics*; *Managing Money*; *Raising Money*; *Paying for College: Practical, Creative Strategies*; *Booms, Bubbles and Busts: The Economic Cycle*; and *How Credit Crises Happen*. She is an economics and personal finance content developer for online educational companies and an author with the Council for Economic Education. She received a B.A. in economics from the University of Michigan and an M.A. in economics from New York University, specializing in statistics and econometrics and international economics.

Photo Credits

Cover Jupiterimages/Brand X Pictures/Thinkstock; back cover, p. 19, multiple interior pages background image iStockphoto/Thinkstock; pp. 4-5 David Young-Wolff/Photographer's Choice/Getty Images; p. 8 Radius Images/Getty Images; p. 14 Lisa F. Young/Shutterstock.com; p. 22 Anna Zielinska/E+/Getty Images; p. 27 JohnKwan/Shutterstock.com; p. 30 Yuri Arcurs/Shutterstock.com; p. 32 Hill Street Studios/Blend Images/Getty Images; p. 36 © iStockphoto.com/fazon1; p. 38 Joos Mind/Taxi/Getty Images; p. 41 Supri Suharjoto/Shutterstock.com; p. 45 Bloomberg/Getty Images; p. 49 Jason Cox/Shutterstock.com; p. 51 Christian Science Monitor/Getty Images.

Designer: Michael Moy; Editor: Andrea Sclarow Paskoff; Photo Researcher: Karen Huang